309432

Don't Forget!

Bonfire Night

Monica Hughes

www.heinemann.co.uk/library
Visit our website to find out more information about **Heinemann Library** books.

To order:
 Phone 44 (0) 1865 888066
 Send a fax to 44 (0) 1865 314091
 Visit the Heinemann Bookshop at www.heinemann.co.uk/library to browse our catalogue and order online.

First published in Great Britain by Heinemann Library, Halley Court, Jordan Hill, Oxford OX2 8EJ, a division of Reed Educational and Professional Publishing Ltd. Heinemann is a registered trademark of Reed Educational and Professional Publishing Ltd.

OXFORD MELBOURNE AUCKLAND JOHANNESBURG BLANTYRE
GABORONE IBADAN PORTSMOUTH NH (USA) CHICAGO

Designed by Joanna Sapwell and StoryBooks
Originated by Ambassador Litho Ltd
Printed in China by Wing King Tong

ISBN 0 431 15401 5 (hardback)   ISBN 0 431 15408 2 (paperback)
06 05 04 03   07 06 05 04 03
10 9 8 7 6 5 4 3 2   10 9 8 7 6 5 4 3 2 1

British Library Cataloguing in Publication Data
Hughes, Monica
        Bonfire Night. – (Don't Forget)
        1. Guy Fawkes Day – Juvenile literature
        I.Title
        394 . 2 '64

Acknowledgements
The Publishers would like to thank the following for permission to reproduce photographs: Bridgeman Art Library p. 17; Collection/Brian Shuel pp. 4, 11, 12, 22, 23, 24; Collections/Keith Fryer p. 13; Collections/Roger Scruton p. 8; Corbis pp. 6, 15, 21, 26; Corbis/Earl Kowall p. 19; Corbis/Jonathan Blair p. 7; Corbis/Martin Jones p. 9; Corbis/Pawel Libera p. 27; Getty Images/Stone pp. 14, 28; Mary Evans Picture Library p. 10; Photodisc pp. 5, 16; Photofusion/Colin Edwards p. 18; Rye Bonfire Society p. 25; Topham Picturepoint p. 29; Trevor Clifford p. 20.

Cover photograph reproduced with permission of Pictures/Clive Sawyer.

Our thanks to Stuart Copeman for his assistance in the preparation of this book.

Every effort has been made to contact copyright holders of any material reproduced in this book. Any omissions will be rectified in subsequent printings if notice is given to the Publishers.

Contents

Words printed in bold letters, **like this**, are explained in the Glossary.

What is Bonfire Night?

A guy burning on a
5 November bonfire

Bonfire Night is a celebration that takes place every year on 5 November. It is also known as Guy Fawkes' night or fireworks' night. Three different things make Bonfire Night special. There is the blazing bonfire that lights up the dark November sky. There is the 'guy' or dummy that sits on the top of the bonfire and is destroyed by the flames. There are fantastic fireworks that add sparkling lights and **sound effects** to the celebrations as they whistle, screech and bang into the air.

Celebrations on 5 November remember an event that happened in 1605. On that date, the lives of King James I and all of his government were saved when a plot to kill

Fireworks on Bonfire Night

them was discovered. The plot was to blow up the Houses of Parliament, and Guy Fawkes was caught in the cellars underneath Parliament with the barrels of gunpowder.

Remember, Remember!

Here is a famous children's rhyme about Guy Fawkes:

Remember, remember the fifth of November
Gunpowder, treason and plot.
I see no reason why gunpowder treason
Should ever be forgot.
Guy Fawkes, Guy Fawkes
'Twas his intent
To blow up the king and the Parliament
Three score *barrels of powder below*
Poor old England to overthrow.
By God's ***providence*** *he was catched*
With a dark lantern and burning match.

The gunpowder plot

The leader of the plot to blow up King James I and his Parliament was not Guy Fawkes but Robert Catesby. His plan was to rent a house next door to the Parliament building then dig an underground tunnel leading to the Houses of Parliament. They would then use gunpowder to blow Parliament up.

They found a house and started to dig a tunnel but then rented a cellar under the Parliament building. They stored 36 barrels of gunpowder in the cellar ready for the **State Opening of Parliament** on 5 November.

An engraving of the members of the gunpowder plot

Yeomen of the Guard at the Tower of London

The plan was discovered because one of the plotters sent a letter to warn a friend not to go to the Opening of Parliament. This letter was shown to the King who thought that it meant that there was a plot to kill him. He ordered that the cellars be searched, and around midnight on 4 November Guy Fawkes and the plot were discovered.

Searching the cellars

Even today the cellars of Parliament are still searched before important occasions like the State Opening of Parliament in case anyone is hiding there. A group of men called the Yeoman of the Guard take part in this private ceremony, which is a reminder of the gunpowder plot. The Yeoman, who are also called Beefeaters, normally look after the Tower of London.

Guy Fawkes

Guy Fawkes was discovered with the barrels of gunpowder. He was not the leader of the plot, but he was an expert with gunpowder. Guy was his nickname, his real name was Guido.

Guido was born in York and went to St Peter's School there. He made friends with two brothers at school, John and Christopher Wright, and years later they were all to become members of the gunpowder plot. When Guido left school he became a soldier. While he was fighting in Spain he became an expert at using gunpowder.

After he was caught, Guy Fawkes was **imprisoned** in the Tower of London and tortured until he gave the names of the other plotters. They were all caught, found

St Peter's School in York as it is today

The Tower of London where Guy Fawkes was imprisoned and tortured.

guilty of **treason** and killed. Guy Fawkes was also killed. Their heads were cut off and left on the top of wooden poles in the centre of London.

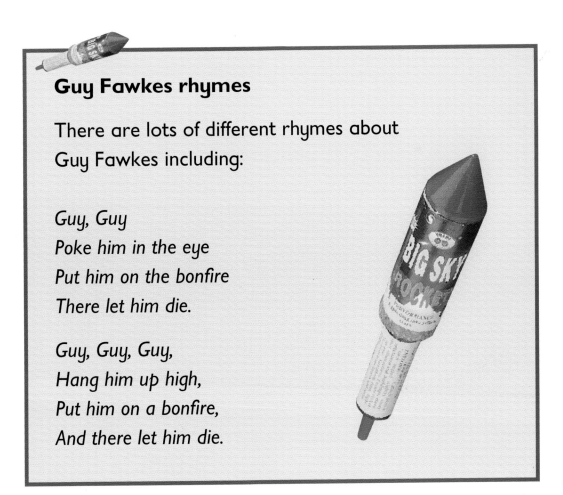

Guy Fawkes rhymes

There are lots of different rhymes about Guy Fawkes including:

Guy, Guy
Poke him in the eye
Put him on the bonfire
There let him die.

Guy, Guy, Guy,
Hang him up high,
Put him on a bonfire,
And there let him die.

Penny for the guy

At one time, in the days leading up to Bonfire Night, groups of children could be seen on street corners asking anyone who passed to give 'A penny for the guy'. The children made a stuffed dummy using old clothes, newspaper and sometimes straw. The dummy often wore a frightening mask and would be sitting in an old pram, go-kart or wheelbarrow. This dummy was their 'guy' and **represented** Guy Fawkes. It would be burnt on the top of the bonfire on 5 November.

An illustration drawn in 1899 called *A Penny for the Guy*

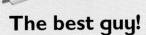

The best guy!

At one time there was great competition between children as to who could make the best guy. **Rival gangs** stuffed old suits for the body, had old shoes for feet, gloves for hands and topped the head with a splendid hat.

Begging for a penny for the guy was a way in which children could collect money for fireworks. Children under 18 are no longer allowed to buy fireworks, so the **custom** of a penny for the guy has begun to die out. Guys are sometimes made in the shape of famous people, and used as a way of collecting money for **charity**.

Ready to ask, 'A penny for the guy?'

11

Mischief night

In some parts of northern England and Scotland the night before Bonfire Night was known as mischief night. On the evening of 4 November young people got up to all sorts of **pranks** and mischief. The **custom** has links with Halloween when mischievous spirits were thought to be around.

A common prank on mischief night was to knock on the front door of a house and run away before anyone came to answer it. Gates would also be removed from their hinges and carried off down the street. Doorknobs would

A Guy Fawkes bonfire ready for 5 November

A parade of a guy on Bonfire Night

be covered in treacle, and eggs would sometimes be thrown as well as bags of flour. However, in some places the pranks were very dangerous. Fires were sometimes started by accident. People have been injured on mischief night and so young people are not now encouraged to take part in it.

Danger!

At one time it was common for teenagers to throw fireworks called **bangers** around on mischief night but this is now illegal. It is a **criminal offence** to throw any kind of firework in the street or a public place. The maximum fine is £5000.

The first bonfires

A flaming bonfire being enjoyed by crowds

Bonfire Night was first celebrated in 1606, on the **anniversary** of the discovery of the plot to kill King James. However, an autumn celebration involving bonfires is much older than this.

The **Celts** had a celebration called 'Samhain' meaning summers end. It took place around the end of October or the beginning of November, the time that Halloween is now celebrated.

The Celts lit huge bonfires and had torchlit processions to celebrate the beginning of the new year. The bonfires were thought to give strength to the sun that was

14

believed to be getting weaker and weaker as winter arrived. They were also thought to frighten away evil spirits that were believed to be around at this time of year.

A man-shaped green figure was often burnt on the autumn bonfires. The model was an offering to the gods and was thought to bring a good harvest for the following year.

A fire juggler

Catherine wheels

An ancient Christian **festival** involving fire and fireworks was held hundreds of years ago in November. It was in memory of St Catherine who was put to death on a spiked wheel. To remind people what happened, a juggler would make wheels of fire appear by whirling lighted torches in the air. Wheel-shaped **firecrackers**, now called Catherine wheels, would also be set off.

 # Fireworks

The first fireworks were made in China nearly two thousand years ago. They were made using pieces of hollow bamboo to hold the gunpowder and were known as 'bamboo **firecrackers**'. Paper tubes later replaced the bamboo. Fireworks were used in **religious ceremonies** in China and the Far East for centuries.

The famous explorer Marco Polo was thought to have brought fireworks to Europe. Florence, a city in Italy, became the place where most fireworks were made. The first recorded use of fireworks in England was at the wedding of King Henry VII in 1486. They were very popular by the time of Henry VIII. Elizabeth I even had a fireworks master to organize the firework displays.

Multicoloured fireworks

An engraving from 1749 of fireworks on the River Thames

These displays could be as long as 183 metres (600 feet) and as high as 27 metres (90 feet). They told stories of great battles or other important events.

The first fireworks were only gold and silver but today every colour imaginable can be seen. There are all kinds of **sound effects** and the fireworks make lots of different shapes in the sky.

Did you know?

More than 100 million fireworks are sold in Britain every year. The same names have been used for fireworks for many years. Some of the most popular are roman candle, mount Vesuvius, silver rain and golden shower. There are also Catherine wheels that spin around and around, and rockets that fly through the air.

17

Firework code

Fireworks may look beautiful but they can be very dangerous. There are some simple safety rules, known as the firework code, which should be followed by everyone using fireworks.

- Never go near or use fireworks without an adult.
- Keep fireworks in a box or tin and only get them out one at a time.
- Keep a bucket of water close by.
- Read and follow the **instructions** for every firework carefully.
- Use a taper or special firework lighter and light the firework at arm's length.
- Direct rocket fireworks well away from **spectators**.
- Never return to re-light a firework even if it seems to have gone out.

Fireworks can be dangerous

Children enjoying sparklers

- Stand well back when fireworks are being lit.
- Keep pets indoors not just on Bonfire Night but on the evenings before and after it.
- Keep a close eye on children and don't give sparklers to very young children.
- Never put fireworks in a pocket.
- Never throw fireworks or fool around with them.

Be safe

It is very common for people to be injured by fireworks. Every year there are more than a thousand accidents and nearly half of those injured are children aged 14 or younger. Sparklers cause more injuries than either **bangers** or air bombs.

Bonfire Night food and drink

There are several special types of food that people enjoy as they gather round a bonfire on a cold and dark 5 November evening.

Potatoes can be baked in the ashes of the fire and roasted chestnuts can also be enjoyed. A sweet sticky cake called Parkin used to be a favourite. It was made with oatmeal, ginger and treacle and is still eaten today. Gingerbread men are sometimes eaten, perhaps because they remind people of Guy Fawkes. Have you ever had a toffee apple? These are apples coated in sticky toffee and eaten off a stick. Different kinds of toffee are also popular.

Food to enjoy on Bonfire Night

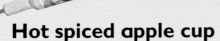

Hot spiced apple cup

This is a warm drink to enjoy outside on Bonfire Night. Mix cranberry juice, apple juice and lemon juice with sugar. Add cinnamon, nutmeg, cloves and allspice, then heat in a pan. Serve in warm mugs with a slice of lemon for decoration.

Fast food in the form of burgers and hot dogs are now common, often served from a large food tent or mobile van. A blazing barbeque is also popular. It can be a warm **focus** on the chilly November evening. Mugs of steaming soup and other hot drinks are also good things to enjoy outside at Bonfire Night.

Children enjoying special treats round the bonfire

Bonfire societies

From about 1700 special bonfire societies were formed to organize events for Bonfire Night. These societies still exist in parts of Sussex and Kent. Each society has its own **traditions** and often have impressive celebrations. People dress up in different fancy costumes such as **Vikings**, pirates and cowboys. They all take part in **processions** lit by flaming torches. Bands play as the procession winds through the streets collecting money for **charity**.

Flaming torches carried by The Cliffe Society in Lewes, Sussex

The Battel Bonfire Boyes

This bonfire society organizes a celebration on the first Saturday in November. Different societies from the area take part in a procession that goes up and down the High Street. The event ends with a huge bonfire and firework display at the original site of the Battle of Hastings.

At Lewes in East Sussex an enormous guy is made and driven through the narrow crowded streets on the back of a truck. The guy may be as big as a house and will often have a barrel of gunpowder under one arm. The guy will not always be made to look like Guy Fawkes. Sometimes they are cartoon characters or politicians. They have even included a 'guy' in the shape of a dinosaur. There is a spectacular firework display and the guy is eventually burnt on a huge bonfire.

A guy dressed as a cowboy at Lewes, Sussex

Burning barrels and boats

In the past, some dangerous games were played at the Bonfire Night celebrations. A kind of relay race was held with barrels full of burning tar. A team of men would gather to carry the burning barrel around the town. Members of the team would wear **protective** gloves and have wet **sacking** over their head and shoulders. The idea was for each man to carry the barrel high above his head and run with it until he could bear the heat no longer. The flaming barrel was then passed to the next member of the team who would run with it until they could hold it no longer. This continued all around the town.

Burning tar barrels at Ottery St Mary, Devon

Flaming boats

At Rye in Sussex, a model of a **galleon** or a wrecked boat forms part of the celebrations. Huge crowds gather to watch as the bonfire and ship are set alight. The flames outline the shape of the ship as the sails and **rigging** catch fire. The burning ship provides a spectacular **backdrop** to the fireworks that follow.

Most places stopped this **custom** because it was thought to be too dangerous but it is still carried on in Ottery St Mary in Devon. On the evening of 5 November crowds gather to watch men carry the flaming barrels around the village.

The burning galleon at Rye

How Bonfire Night has changed

Immediately after the gunpowder plot had been discovered the people of London celebrated because the life of the king had been saved. At that time lighting bonfires was the most common way for people to celebrate. The following year, Parliament passed a law that made 5 November a **public holiday**. This law was in place until 1859.

Bonfire Night celebrations have changed over the years. Small bonfires in back gardens can cause accidents. So large bonfires, organized for the whole community and properly **supervised**, are now more popular.

Two hundred-year-old picture of fireworks on the River Thames

Fireworks are popular at many celebrations

In the past, children would let off fireworks by themselves. But, because they are so dangerous, fireworks can now only be sold to people aged 18 years or over. Today this means that most children will go to an organized fireworks display. They are a spectacular part of the celebrations with large, long-lasting fireworks.

Did you know?

At one time thanksgiving services were held in churches all over the country on 5 November. They were held as a reminder that King James' life had been saved when the gunpowder plot was discovered. Church bells were rung and **cannons** fired as part of the celebrations.

Bonfire Night around the world

Bonfire Night is not only celebrated in Britain. At one time it was common in Canada and New England in the USA.

In New Zealand it is celebrated in much the same way as it is in Britain. Children are told the true story of Guy Fawkes and the gunpowder plot, even though it happened thousands of miles from their country. Firework displays are organized by school and **community** groups but tend to be less elaborate than in Britain. Bonfires are popular but there is less of making and burning 'guys'.

New Year fireworks over Sydney, Australia

Bangers exploding behind the dragon at Chinese New Year

At one time Bonfire Night in Australia was observed by nearly everyone all over the country. There were family and street celebrations that included bonfires and fireworks. Gradually things have changed, and now it is almost impossible to buy fireworks directly from shops in most parts of Australia. However, public displays are still sometimes held.

Fireworks around the world

Fireworks and bonfires are used in many celebrations around the world. Fireworks are popular especially when celebrating **Chinese New Year** and **Divali**. Bonfires and fireworks were used all over the world to celebrate the year 2000 and the new **millennium**.

29

Glossary

anniversary same date as something that happened in the past

bangers fireworks that make a loud noise

backdrop scene at the back of a performance

cannons large heavy guns

Celts people who lived in ancient Britain before the Romans

charity help given to people and animals in need

Chinese New Year Chinese celebrations to mark the start of their New Year

community groups of people living in the same area

criminal offence something done that breaks the law

custom usual way of doing things

Divali Hindu and Sikh celebration to mark the start of their New Year

festival special celebration

firecrackers fireworks

focus centre of attention

galleon large sailing ship with three masts

imprisoned put in prison

instructions words explaining how to do something

millennium period of a thousand years

pranks tricks played on someone

processions groups of people walking along a set route

protective keeping safe from harm

providence care and protection

public holiday holiday for most people

religious ceremonies formal acts that are part of worship

represented stood for

rigging ropes that hold up a ship's sails

rival gangs groups of people who compete against each other

sacking strong cloth used to make sacks

sound effects noises that make something more realistic

spectators people who watch an event

State Opening of Parliament formal ceremony at the beginning of a new period of government

supervised watched and taken care of

three score three times twenty, which equals 60

traditions old customs and ceremonies

treason crime against the country in which you live

Vikings people from northern Europe who invaded England long ago

Index

Titles in the *Don't Forget* series:

Hardback   0 431 15401 5

Hardback   0 431 15403 1

Hardback   0 431 15405 8

Hardback   0 431 15400 7

Hardback   0 431 15404 X

Hardback   0 431 15402 3

Find out about other Heinemann titles on our website www.heinemann.co.uk/library